THE STORY
OF GEORGE WASHINGTON

THE STORY OF
GEORGE
WASHINGTON

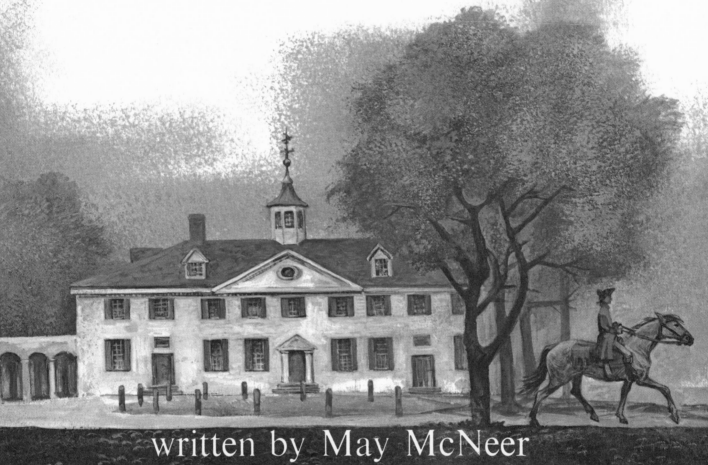

written by May McNeer
pictures by Lynd Ward

ABINGDON
Nashville • New York

Copyright © 1973 by Abingdon Press
All rights reserved
Manufactured by the Parthenon
Press, Nashville, Tennessee,
United States of America

Library of Congress Cataloging in Publication Data

McNeer, May Yonge, 1902-
The story of George Washington.

SUMMARY: A brief and easy-to-read biography of the
first President of the United States.
1. Washington, George, Pres. U. S., 1732-1799—
Juvenile literature. [1. Washington, George, Pres.
U.S., 1732-1799. 2. Presidents] I. Ward, Lynd
Kendall, 1905-   illus. II. Title.
E312.66.M15   973.4'1'0924 [B] [92]   72-12610

ISBN 0-687-39685-9

THE STORY OF GEORGE WASHINGTON
was prepared with the cooperation
and the gracious assistance of

*The Mount Vernon Ladies' Association of
the Union
Mount Vernon, Virginia*

and is published with their approval

A farm boy could ride his horse beside a swift flowing river. With his dogs racing ahead he could ride into deep woods and out again. He could feel the wind blow his hair. As the sun's red face sank behind tall trees, he could gallop home through his father's fields.

George Washington was such a farm boy. He had been born on a farm near Bridges Creek. His birthday was February 22, 1732. When he was three his family moved to another farm. This one later became a large estate named Mount Vernon. George Washington lived there until he was about six. Then the Washingtons moved again, this time to Ferry Farm near Fredericksburg.

All the farms on which George Washington lived were in the colony of Virginia.

At Ferry Farm he sat down to supper at night with his father, Augustine, his mother, Mary, his three younger brothers, and his sister. George had two older half-brothers, the sons of his father's first wife. These two older brothers did not live with the family at Ferry Farm.

George grew tall and strong, but no one knows whether he went to school in the town. Perhaps he had lessons from a teacher who lived nearby? Copy books in which he wrote as a young boy show that he was taught many things. All his life George read books and kept on learning.

When George was eleven his father died. Four years later he went to live with his older half-brother, Lawrence. Ann Washington, Lawrence's wife, was kin to Lord Fairfax. George was interested in listening to the talk of important men who visited Mount Vernon.

He learned how to mark the boundaries of land, and, when he grew older, George went with others to western Virginia to survey wild lands owned by Lord Fairfax.

No one could ride a horse or hunt as well as George Washington. After a while he learned to dance, play card games, and enjoy plays.

When Lawrence fell ill, he asked George to go with him to the island of Barbados. The warm sun would surely make him well. Instead, he grew worse. George also was very ill there. After they were at home again at Mount Vernon, Lawrence died. His only child did not live long after him, and Lawrence's wife, Ann, moved away. She rented the estate to George, who was to inherit it after her.

And so George Washington became master of Mount Vernon, one of the larger plantations in the colony.

Virginia was one of the thirteen American colonies belonging to England and ruled by King George III. Virginia had a governor, appointed by the king. There was a House of Burgesses, a group of men elected by the people, to run the colony under the governor. Williamsburg was the capital of the government in Virginia.

In Virginia men had formed a small army, a militia, to protect the colonists. Washington became a major in the militia. Several times he led soldiers into western forests to fight Frenchmen and Indians.

Washington became a colonel in the militia and joined British General Edward Braddock on a march into the wilderness to the west.

General Braddock meant to force the French to go back
north to Canada. He did not realize that English troops in
red coats would make easy targets for arrows and bullets.
French and Indian fighters attacked the British fiercely. The
battle was lost and General Braddock was killed.

15

Colonel Washington took command and brought the men safely home. He was praised for his skill and bravery and put in charge of the military defense of Virginia.

When the French did return to the north, Washington became a farmer again. He married a widow, Mrs. Martha Custis. With her two children, Jack and Patsy Custis, Martha came to live at Mount Vernon. George Washington treated Jack and Patsy as if they were his own children. He sent to England for toys for them and invited friends to bring their children to play at Mount Vernon.

George Washington was a member of the Church of England, later the Episcopal Church. He served his church as vestryman and then as a warden, and he served his community as a justice of the peace. The people of his own county elected him to represent them in the House of Burgesses.

From time to time he went to Williamsburg to meet with the Burgesses. Sometimes Mrs. Washington and the children went with him. They rode in the big family coach, drawn by six horses.

As the months and years passed, there were changes in life at Mount Vernon. When Patsy was seventeen her parents were saddened by her long illness and death. In that same year Jack Custis left college and was married to Nelly Calvert of Maryland.

17

There were changes in the lives of all the American colonists. The people of the colonies did not like being told what to do by the king in far-off England. They did not want to pay extra taxes on tea and other goods sent from England. They wished to make their own laws. In Boston Harbor citizens dressed as Indians dumped boxes of tea from British ships into the water. This was called "The Boston Tea Party." After that a large force of British soldiers was sent to Boston. This made the colonists very angry.

In Virginia meetings were held to talk about unjust taxes. Patrick Henry made a speech, shouting "Give me liberty, or give me death!" Washington was quiet and dignified and did not make speeches like that. Yet his opinions were often asked.

He was elected as one of seven to go from Virginia to the First Continental Congress in Philadelphia in 1774. This congress was the first meeting of men from the different colonies, gathered to discuss their problems. Only one colony, Georgia, did not send anyone.

In April, 1775, patriots stood their ground with muskets
against British troops in Lexington and at Concord Bridge
in the Massachusetts colony. In that summer the Second Continental Congress chose George Washington to be the general
and commander in chief of the army. Washington left for
Massachusetts to take command of the army there.

The Declaration of Independence was adopted by Congress on July 4, 1776. Americans cheered, and men came from all the colonies to join the new army.

It was not easy for General Washington to make a trained army of farmers and townsmen. Yet the general knew that all these men were brave. They wanted their country to be free. He was glad to see frontiersmen coming to him with their long rifles. They were expert marksmen.

Many battles were fought between the new Continental Army and the British. Some were won by the Americans, but at first more were lost. By autumn Washington's men were cold, sick, and hungry. They retreated southward from battles in New York until they reached Pennsylvania.

Later that year a great victory was won. It was Christmas Eve. Hessian mercenaries were celebrating in Trenton, New Jersey. The mercenaries had been hired by the British to help them fight the war. In darkness of night, General Washington brought his army by rowboat across the ice-choked Delaware to surprise the enemy. That battle was won, and there were to be others.

Then came the hardest time of the war. Washington's army suffered terribly as it camped in the snow at Valley Forge after the British took Philadelphia.

When General Gilbert Lafayette of France came to join the American forces, General Washington was glad to have him on his staff. The two men became lifelong friends.

At the important battle of Yorktown, Virginia, French and American troops stood side by side. The French fleet kept British ships from coming to the aid of their own army. The British General Charles Cornwallis surrendered to General Washington. The war was not over. Yet peace would come before long.

When the war ended, General Washington met with his officers at Fraunces Tavern in New York. The men were in tears as he told them farewell. Then George Washington rode home to his beloved Mount Vernon. He arrived on Christmas Eve, 1783.

Waiting with Martha to welcome the general back to Mount Vernon were two young children. Jack Custis had died of a fever, leaving his widow with four children. Their mother allowed the two youngest to live with Martha and George Washington. The children's names were Washington and Nelly Custis.

General Washington soon added more land to his plantation. Every day he rode out to oversee the work. Sometimes
little Washington Custis, known affectionately as "Tub," rode
with him on a pony. Of an evening the general enjoyed listening to Nelly Custis playing the spinet.

Mount Vernon was a small village in itself. Mrs. Washington was kept busy directing the sewing, spinning, cooking,
and the many other tasks. And the General's Lady was a
gracious hostess to the stream of guests in their home.

When the time came to elect the first President of the United States, who but George Washington could be chosen? He had served his country well in wartime. Now he would become a great leader in peace.

President Washington took office in New York City. His first speech was made from a porch at Federal Hall. Since the President must live in New York, Martha went there with the grandchildren, little Washington and Nelly Custis. The President's home became the center of the social life of the country.

The Constitution had been written for the new nation to make a government built on justice. The Bill of Rights was added to it to protect the rights of citizens. It was some time before all the states signed it. But at last they did, to make one nation, the United States of America.

The President had the huge task of setting up a democratic government and making it work. Some of the men helping to run the country did not agree with the President's plans or his way of doing things. Still, it was George Washington who had the trust of the people.

Before George Washington was elected President for a second time, the government had been moved from New York to Philadelphia. But a new city, to be the capital of the new nation, was being built on the shore of the Potomac River. It was named Washington, District of Columbia. In 1793 the President came there to lay the cornerstone of the Capitol building, where Congress still meets.

During his second term as President, Washington rode through the South in his large coach, pulled by four horses. He had already made such a tour in New England. He wanted to know the people of all the states. Everywhere he went he was greeted with affection and cheers.

When it was time for the next election, Washington refused
to be President again. After giving so many years to his country, he wished to go home and live at Mount Vernon. The
life there was busier than ever before. Visitors came, even
from across the seas, to talk with George Washington.

35

On December 12, in 1799, Washington rode around his
farms in sleet and snow. The next day he became ill, and
he lived only until ten o'clock in the evening on December 14.

Many large plantation owners had slaves. In his will George Washington freed the slaves who had worked for him.

He was buried at Mount Vernon. Two and a half years later, his wife was laid to rest near him.

America mourned for George Washington. In war he had led the colonies to freedom. In peace he had done more than any other to make a strong and free United States of America.

GLOSSARY

Some of the words listed below have several meanings. This glossary attempts to define a word as it is used in THE STORY OF GEORGE WASHINGTON.

Bill of Rights

The list of freedoms and rights claimed by every U.S. citizen. (The Bill of Rights is the name given to the first ten amendments of the U.S. Constitution.)

boundary, boundaries

The line or lines marking the end of a piece of land belonging to a person or a country.

Burgess, House of Burgesses

A person elected to represent a town or county in the government. The House of Burgesses in Virginia was the group elected by the people to represent the counties.

capital

The town or city where the main government of a county, state, or country is located.

capitol

In each state, the main building where the state government meets; in Washington, D.C., the building where the Congress meets.

citizen

A person living in a country; one who owes allegiance (loyalty) to that country's government and expects its protection.

colonel

An officer in the Army.

colonist, colonists

A person or the people who lived in the thirteen colonies in the early days of America.

colony

A group of people who leave their own country (the place where they were born) and go to form a new community or town, sometimes in a distant land, who still must obey the laws of the king or the government of the homeland.

command

To lead or direct; to be in charge of a group.

38

commander

One who leads or directs.

community

A group of homes, or farms, and small businesses.

Congress

A group of people elected to represent their states in the main government of the land; or, the meeting of senators and representatives elected by the people.

constitution

The list of rules or laws by which the country is governed.

Continental Congress

The meeting of the men who represented the original thirteen colonies.

cornerstone

A stone forming part of a corner of a building. The laying of this stone in an important building is an impressive ceremony. Often the stone is hollow and in it are placed small relics and certain documents.

Declaration of Independence

The public announcement by which the thirteen colonies stated their intention to be free of the British rule.

democratic

The kind of government which favors equal treatment of all citizens.

estate

A piece of property; lands and buildings.

frontiersman

A person living far away from the settlement or town where others live.

general

An officer of the highest grade in the Army.

half-brother

One who has the same father as you but a different mother; or, one who has the same mother as you but a different father.

Hessian

A person who was born or lived in Hesse (Germany).

House of Burgesses

A group of men elected by the people from the counties in colonial Virginia. The group met regularly to discuss the laws and the rights of the colonists.

independent

Not controlled or ruled by others; free.

justice of the peace
An officer or judge of a town or community; one who handles local matters, fees, etc.

major
An officer in the Army.

marksman, marksmen
A man or men trained to shoot straight.

mercenaries
Soldiers who fight just for the pay and not from a sense of loyalty or duty.

military
The organization of armed forces, soldiers and equipment.

militia
A group of citizens who get together for protection against an enemy.

mourn, mourned
To be sorry or sad; to have expressed sorrow or sadness.

muskets
Large guns carried by soldiers.

patriot
One who loves his country.

plantation
A farm or estate, usually large enough to require many workers to plant and harvest crops.

retreat, retreated
To leave quickly from a dangerous place or situation; to have done this.

Rights, Bill of
The list of freedoms and rights claimed by citizens of the U.S. (The Bill of Rights is the name given to the first ten amendments to the U.S. Constitution.)

slave
One whose life and work are under the absolute control of another person.

staff
A group of people who work together under a commander or director.

survey
To measure and mark boundary lines.

vestryman
One of the officials who handle the affairs of an Episcopal church.

warden
The principal officer handling the affairs of an Episcopal church.

Note: the actual date of Washington's birth was February 11, but through a calendar revision it became February 22, the date celebrated through the years.